SSI Monograph

HARD POWER AND SOFT POWER: THE UTILITY OF MILITARY FORCE AS AN INSTRUMENT OF POLICY IN THE 21ST CENTURY

Colin S. Gray

April 2011

*****

Comments pertaining to this report are invited and should be forwarded to: Director, Strategic Studies Institute, U.S. Army War College, 632 Wright Ave, Carlisle, PA 17013-5046.

*****

The Strategic Studies Institute publishes a monthly e-mail newsletter to update the national security community on the research of our analysts, recent and forthcoming publications, and upcoming conferences sponsored by the Institute. Each newsletter also provides a strategic commentary by one of our research analysts. If you are interested in receiving this newsletter, please subscribe on the SSI website at *www.StrategicStudiesInstitute. army.mil/ newsletter/.*

ISBN 978-1-257-62724-0
Cover and promotional text (c) 2011 Booklife
Commercial reprint, April 2011

FOREWORD

The concept of soft power, that is the influence attained through the co-option of foreigners by the attractiveness of our values, ideas, and practices, understandably has great appeal. Soft power is much cheaper than the hard power of military force, and it is more compatible with the culture of a principally liberal American society. All too often, military force seems to fail as an instrument of policy and, as a consequence, it invites the view that it is becoming obsolescent and even anachronistic.

Dr. Colin Gray subjects hard and soft power to close critical scrutiny and finds that the latter is significantly misunderstood and, as a consequence, misassessed as a substitute for the threat or use of military force. Each kind of power has its limitations, but the obvious and familiar challenges characteristic of military force do not mean that therefore soft power should be our policy instrument of choice. The author warns against expecting too much of soft power.

DOUGLAS C. LOVELACE, JR.
Director
Strategic Studies Institute

ABOUT THE AUTHOR

COLIN S. GRAY is Professor of International Politics and Strategic Studies at the University of Reading, England. He worked at the International Institute for Strategic Studies (London), and at Hudson Institute (Croton-on-Hudson, NY) before founding the National Institute for Public Policy, a defense-oriented think tank in the Washington, DC, area. Dr. Gray served for 5 years in the Reagan administration on the President's General Advisory Committee on Arms Control and Disarmament. He has served as an adviser to both the U.S. and British governments (he has dual citizenship). His government work has included studies of nuclear strategy, arms control, maritime strategy, space strategy and the use of special forces. Dr. Gray has written 24 books, including: *The Sheriff: America's Defense of the New World Order* (University Press of Kentucky, 2004); *Another Bloody Century: Future Warfare* (Weidenfeld and Nicolson, 2005); *Strategy and History: Essays on Theory and Practice* (Routledge, 2007; Potomac Books, 2009); *National Security Dilemmas: Challenges and Opportunities* (Potomac Books, 2009); and *The Strategy Bridge: Theory for Practice* (Oxford University Press, 2010). His next book will be *Airpower for Strategic Effect*. Dr. Gray is a graduate of the Universities of Manchester and Oxford.

SUMMARY

Power is one of the more contestable concepts in political theory, but it is conventional and convenient to define it as "the ability to effect the outcomes you want and, if necessary, to change the behavior of others to make this happen." (Joseph S. Nye, Jr.) In recent decades, scholars and commentators have chosen to distinguish between two kinds of power, "hard" and "soft." The former, hard power, is achieved through military threat or use, and by means of economic menace or reward. The latter, soft power, is the ability to have influence by co-opting others to share some of one's values and, as a consequence, to share some key elements on one's agenda for international order and security. Whereas hard power obliges its addressees to consider their interests in terms mainly of calculable costs and benefits, principally the former, soft power works through the persuasive potency of ideas that foreigners find attractive. The nominal promise in this logic is obvious. Plainly, it is highly desirable if much of the world external to America wants, or can be brought to want, a great deal of what America happens to favor also. Coalitions of the genuinely willing have to be vastly superior to the alternatives.

Unfortunately, although the concept of American soft power is true gold in theory, in practice it is not so valuable. Ironically, the empirical truth behind the attractive concept is just sufficient to mislead policymakers and grand strategists. Not only do Americans want to believe that the soft power of their civilization and culture is truly potent, we are all but programmed by our enculturation to assume that the American story and its values do and should have what amounts to missionary merit that ought to be universal. American culture is so powerful a programmer that it can be difficult for Americans to empathize with, or even understand, the somewhat different values and their implications held deeply abroad. The idea is popular, even possibly authoritative, among Americans that ours is not just an "ordinary country," but instead is a country both exceptionally blessed (by divine intent) and, as a consequence, exceptionally obliged to lead Mankind. When national exceptionalism is not merely a proposition, but is more akin to an iconic item of faith, it is difficult for usually balanced American minds to consider the potential of their soft power without rose-tinted spectacles. And the problem is that they are somewhat correct. American values, broadly speaking "the American way," to hazard a large project in reductionism, are indeed attractive beyond America's frontiers and have some utility for U.S. policy. But there are serious limitations to the worth of the concept of soft power, especially as it might be thought of as an instrument of policy. To date, the idea of soft power has not been subjected to a sufficiently critical forensic examination. In particular, the relation of the soft power of attraction and persuasion to the hard power of coercion urgently requires more rigorous examination than it has received thus far.

When considered closely, the subject of soft power and its implications for the hard power of military force reveals a number of plausible working propositions that have noteworthy meaning for U.S. policy and strategy.

1. Hard military threat and use are more difficult to employ today than was the case in the past, in part because of the relatively recent growth in popular

respect for universal humanitarian values. However, this greater difficulty does not mean that military force has lost its distinctive ability to secure some political decisions. The quality of justification required for the use of force has risen, which means that the policy domain for military relevance has diminished, but has by no means disappeared.

2. The political and other contexts for the use of force today do not offer authoritative guidance for the future. History is not reliably linear. To know the 2000s is not necessarily to know the 2010s.

3. The utility of military force is not a fixed metric value, either universally or for the United States. The utility of force varies with culture and circumstance, *inter alia*. It is not some free-floating objective calculable truth.

4. For both good and for ill, ethical codes are adapted and applied under the pressure of more or less stressful circumstances, and tend to be significantly situational in practice. This is simply the way things are and have always been. What a state licenses or tolerates by way of military behavior effected in its name depends to a degree on how desperate and determined are its policymakers and strategists.

5. War involves warfare, which means military force, which means violence that causes damage, injury, and death. Some of the debate on military force and its control fails to come to grips with the bloody reality, chaos, and friction that is in the very nature of warfare. Worthy and important efforts to limit conduct in warfare cannot avoid accepting the inherent nastiness of the subject. War may be necessary and it should be restrained in its conduct, but withal it is by definition illiberally violent behavior.

6. By and large, soft power should not be thought of as an instrument of policy. America is what it is, and the ability of Washington to project its favored "narrative(s)" is heavily constrained. Cultural diplomacy and the like are hugely mortgaged by foreigners' own assessments of their interests. And a notable dimension of culture is local, which means that efforts to project American ways risk fueling "blow-back."

7. Soft power cannot sensibly be regarded as a substantial alternative to hard military power. Familiarity with the concept alone encourages the fallacy that hard and soft power have roughly equivalent weight and utility. An illusion of broad policy choice is thus fostered, when in fact effective choices are severely constrained.

8. An important inherent weakness of soft power as an instrument of policy is that it utterly depends upon the uncoerced choices of foreigners. Sometimes their preferences will be compatible with ours, but scarcely less often they will not be. Interests and cultures do differ.

9. Soft power tends to be either so easy to exercise that it is probably in little need of a policy push, being essentially preexistent, or too difficult to achieve because local interests, or culture, or both, deny it political traction.

10. Hard and soft power should be complementary, though often they are not entirely so. U.S. national style, reflecting the full array of American values as a hegemonic power, has been known to give some cultural and hence political offense abroad, even among objective allies and other friends. Whereas competent strategy enables hard military power to be all, or most of what it can be, soft power does not lend itself readily to strategic direction.

11. Provided the different natures of hard and soft power are understood — the critical distinguishing factor being coercion versus attraction — it is appropriate to regard the two kinds of power as mutual enablers. However, theirs is an unequal relationship. The greater attractiveness of soft power is more than offset in political utility by its inherent unsuitability for policy direction and control.

From all the factors above, it follows that military force will long remain an essential instrument of policy. That said, popular enthusiasm in Western societies for the placing of serious restraints on the use of force can threaten the policy utility of the military. The ill consequences of America's much-manifested difficulty in thinking and behaving strategically are augmented perilously when unwarranted faith is placed upon soft power that inherently is resistant to strategic direction. Although it is highly appropriate to be skeptical of the policy utility of soft power, such skepticism must not be interpreted as implicit advice to threaten or resort to military force with scant reference to moral standards. Not only is it right in an absolute sense, it is also expedient to seek, seize, and hold the moral high ground. There can be significant strategic advantage in moral advantage — to risk sounding cynical. Finally, it is essential to recognize that soft power tends to work well when America scarcely has need of it, but the more challenging contexts for national security require the mailed fist, even if it is cushioned, but not concealed, by a glove of political and ethical restraint.

HARD POWER AND SOFT POWER: THE UTILITY OF MILITARY FORCE AS AN INSTRUMENT OF POLICY IN THE 21ST CENTURY

Simply put, power is the ability to effect the outcomes you want, and if necessary, to change the behavior of others to make this happen.

Joseph S. Nye Jr., 2002[1]

Hard times make for soft principles.

Gavin Lyall, 1993[2]

INTRODUCTION: RUST ON THE MAILED FIST?

Fighting is the core competency of the soldier; he is a specialist in violence. While armed forces can serve many purposes, what defines them uniquely is their ability to damage things and injure or kill people as a legitimate instrument of the polity. When functioning under the authority of law to advance or protect the political interests of a security community, the soldier can be said to threaten or execute force rather than violence.[3] This distinction in language, and even in concept, is apt to be clearer in principle than it is in practice, particularly if one is on the receiving end.

The main purpose of this analysis is to consider the relevance of military power today as well as for tomorrow. This is a subject that should give one pause before claiming a confident understanding of it. Major trends seem clear enough, but will they continue? The frequency with which history shows a liking for irony suggests that the future context for military power may be unlike that of today, in good part because the contemporary situation contains features that will be repudiated in the future in some mixture of thought, word, and deed. The course of history assuredly reveals that events must advance from what preceded them, which is why defense analysis, especially if it seeks to peer into the future, must honor chronology. But the chronology of historical narrative may obscure the traps of nonlinearity. What we know for certain about the 21st century is that we know little of detail with total assurance. Moreover, even broad trends that appear to have unstoppable momentum are not to be trusted to deliver on their obvious promise.

History must be our guide, if only because nothing else is accessible. Unfortunately, the past as it is interpreted in the history written by historians provides anything but a reliable compass. Argument either by historical analogy, or at the least with illustration by historical anecdote claimed to be pertinent, is the rule, not the exception, in political discourse.[4] This is scarcely surprising, since today is by definition both brief and unstable, while the future by definition is blank. All that is available as an evidential base for our political and strategic guidance is a past that cannot be recovered faithfully, even by those who seek honestly to do so, with the result that the past is mediated by historians. Since many facts do not speak with total clarity for themselves, they have to be interpreted by historians, amateur and professional.[5] A factually reliable chronicle of an obviously major episode in the recent past, World War II say, or the Cold War, is easier to assemble than is a theory, or rather an explanation, which makes thoroughly persuasive sense of the subject at issue.

All too obviously, this monograph cannot and should not seek to build from a clean slate. Of course one seeks truth, but already there is a great deal that claims to be that rare commodity out there, both in the marketplace of popular ideas and also in the laws, rules, customs, norms, and policies currently extant and indeed variably authoritative. Readers scarcely need reminding that my subject is not at all *terra incognita*. In point of fact, the very strength of the contemporary Western currency of beliefs and rules is itself something of a challenge to this particular project. Moreover, the political, legal, and cultural authority of some attitudes that now are dominant can hardly be doubted. Unfortunately, the subject in need of debate for a more prudent understanding is neither the identity nor the desirability of current practice. Rather, it is the overriding issue of the validity of assuming that present contexts determining what is widely believed to be the utility or disutility of force have authority for the future.

For the educational purposes of this monograph, I need to be more respectful of some politically incorrect arguments than is usual, to break some culturally attractive conceptual crockery, and generally to be less than tolerant of some fashionable assumptions and theories. Possibly contrary to appearances, the purpose here is constructive and not destructive for its own sake. But, as the old excuse for atrocity declares, "One cannot make an omelette without breaking eggs."

The plan of attack for this inquiry is to examine the question of the utility of force in the 21st century through the lenses that 11 propositions provide. They differ in focus and attitude, and fairly can be judged to include the correct, the incorrect, the correct but misleading, and the incorrect but enlightening. They have been selected and exploited for their forensic value, not their close fit with what this author believes to be sound. Agreement, disagreement, and partial conditional agreement are registered as best fits the case. The coda comprises a holistic argument in the form of a set of concluding points that have more or less explicit meaning for policy, strategy, and tactics. These conclusions express the outcome to the deliberately granular analyses in the main body of discussion.

11 PROPOSITIONS

1. Military force has less utility as an instrument of policy in the 21st century than it did in times past, even recent times past.

This claim is popular today. The contemporary evidence in its support appears persuasive, and there is no shortage of theory to explain why it should be true. But all that glitters may not be gold, as this monograph will suggest. Commentators and theorists always have trouble distinguishing stand-alone events and episodes from trends. The analogy with climatology is almost too persuasive. In truth, it is a poor journalist or scholar who is unable to show that current conditions — political, strategic, or meteorological — are not indicative of a trend or two, be they welcome or otherwise. There tends to be fame and fortune in the notice that signally good or bad news (it may not much matter which), colorfully conveyed, attracts.

Since all theorists have historical and other coordinates in time, place, and circumstance, so too must their theories bear some greater or lesser imprint of the contexts of their authors. When married to the apparently irresistible human weakness for favoring the relative significance of the present, the widespread attractions of the idea of progress tend to produce ahistorical prognoses of the declining utility of force. Americans (or Britons) who argue today that military force is much less useful a tool for policy than used to be the case, may be making one or more among several candidate claims. Specifically, whether or not they themselves realize it, they could be suggesting any of the following (and this is only a modest selection among the options possible):

a. Globally, for all potential belligerents, military force is of declining utility.

b. Military force is not as useful as was the case, even quite recently, for some security communities, but not for others.

c. Military force is not as useful in wars wherein the warfare is largely of an irregular character as it is in others wherein a customary style of combat dominates. Because today and in the "forseeable future" an irregular character to warfare is, and is expected to be, predominant, military force now is at a heavy discount.[6]

There is much to recommend the three options just offered, but there is a serious possibility that the measure of truth that each contains is more than balanced by its ability to mislead. The first option, ironically, is unsound despite the fact that it is correct and somewhat plausible. Specifically, the now near-instant global access to information enabled by information technology (IT) and space systems, both encourage and discourage the use of force, when force is regarded as a performance for global political (and moral) theater. The global media market that delights in recording atrocities, real or merely claimed, does not necessarily discourage such happenings. On the contrary, the global IT that feeds material for the activation of consciences around the world provides just the marketing assets that some belligerents crave in their demand for attention. We need to beware of theorizing about a context that while truly global, is less than universally common in its meaning.[7]

The second option may well be true, but it might have merit only as a judgment on particular discretionary choices at particular times and places. When military force does not succeed in supporting the goals in its political guidance, it is only reasonable to claim that such force proved less than adequately useful. However, it may well be that the fault lay with the political mission assigned, possibly with the strategy (if any, worthy of the label) attempted, or with a military instrument unable to perform effectively in the field for a number of reasons largely internal to itself. Conflicts and wars can be complex phenomena, as can international relations much more broadly; this means that one should not rush to judgment on the question of the utility or disutility of military force.

The third option suggests that military force may be losing its relative value because it is counterproductive or otherwise ineffective in warfare of an irregular character. This argument can be illustrated by the currently fashionable claim to the effect that we cannot kill our way to victory in Afghanistan. This option is problematic in at least two principal respects. First, it could be less true than it is popular to acknowledge. Second, even if it is as true as its host of adherents today maintain, it is less than self-evident that the conflicts, wars, and warfare of tomorrow will share a character that does not privilege military power among the tools of grand strategy.

Notwithstanding the skeptical notes just struck, plainly the thesis that military power is less useful today than yesterday has much to recommend it. That said, there is much wisdom in the words of Supreme Court Justice Oliver Wendell Holmes, when he advised famously that "[g]eneral propositions do not decide concrete cases."[8] Although this monograph is seeking some general truth about the utility of military force in the 21st century, it is acutely alert to the potential peril of confusing a few concrete cases with irrefutable evidence of a fully matured truth. An American failure to use military force in ways that proved successful in Iraq and Afghanistan, should that be one's current verdict, may have no justification in other episodes of belligerency. Those "concrete cases" may speak only for themselves. They may say little about the strategic value of military force against other belligerents both today and tomorrow, and also as employed by the United States and Britain at other times and in other places and circumstances. Nonetheless, it would be irresponsible in the extreme to attempt to dismiss recent nonuse-of-force prescriptions as harbingers of conflict in a century that is barely 10 years old. We simply do not know what this century will bring.

It is helpful to approach the question of the disutility of military force, that is, quintessential "hard power," with reference to constraints and disincentives. The proposition that military force has lost some, perhaps much, of its usefulness as an instrument of policy is broadly supported by four apparently persuasive claims: two are best categorized under the banner of constraints, and two under that of disincentives.

The content of the constraints basket can be summarized in the twin judgments that the use of military force now entails costs that are much too high, and secures rewards that are unduly meager. The familiar cost-benefit discriminator lends itself to casual deployment that undercuts the case for military action today. When Americans in search of revenge for honor affronted and pain suffered have largely quenched their thirst (as over September 11, 2001 [9/11]), liberal values tend to reappear from the bunker wherein they hid for a while, and the public recalls what it does not like about warfare. War means warfare, *inter alia*, and warfare means death, destruction, and taxes. The conduct of warfare inherently is illiberal behavior, no matter how noble or even inalienable the political (and moral) cause of the moment. The nastiness of war, any war, can be justified in our culture only in terms of its consequential, not its expressive, rewards. The consequences of war and warfare plausibly have to be weighed with the cost-benefit verdict plainly showing as positive for us and our values. When such is not obviously the result, then the cost-benefit books do not balance, let alone show a healthy imbalance for the "right."

In the first decade of this century, America waged warfare that has been unmistakably shy of some approximation of victory. Moreover, the moral climate for contemporary political behavior (warfare is political behavior), has been singularly unpermissive of what allegedly appears as the gratuitous use of military force. Military action, even precisely targeted military action, is portrayed as atrocity by a now globalized media. Writing in the late 1990s, Michael Ignatieff explained the contemporary context for the use of force as follows:

> The world is not becoming more chaotic or violent, although our failure to understand and act makes

it seem so. Nor has the world become more callous. Weak as the narrative of compassion and moral commitment may be, it is infinitely stronger than it was only fifty years ago. We are scarcely aware of the extent to which our moral imagination has been transformed since 1945 by the growth of a language and practice of moral universalism, expressed above all in a shared human rights culture. Television in its turn makes it harder to sustain indifference or ignorance.[9]

Today there is a political and moral battle that inherently is hard to win when one conducts warfare against enemies who hide, yet fight "amongst the people," and are able to decline to do battle of a kind where they might be defeated swiftly and decisively.[10]

When we now consider the matter of disincentives to resort to military force, it follows all too naturally from the previous discussion of constraints that two negative considerations are apt to dominate the field of policy debate. First, so the argument goes, today there is less to gain by the use of military power, even if such use is strategically successful. Second, it can be suggested plausibly that the risks of the resort to military force are significantly different than used to be the case. War remains in principle the servant of the national interest, just as it is still properly held to be the legitimate last resort of the polity. But, increasingly so it would seem, warfare also needs to be "lawfare."[11] Whether or not the national interest might be advanced or protected by force, and whether or not the polity deems itself to be in a situation of "last resort," war today requires persuasive legal justification.[12] Efforts to provide that justification are likely to be more or less challengeable. The legal and legalistic argument will carry a heavy burden of moral baggage, and this weight will likely have practical implications for the conduct and consequences of the warfare. War is always a gamble, a risky endeavor, as Carl von Clausewitz sought to emphasize.[13] For today and prospectively tomorrow, the context includes a now global, attentive, and skeptical news media, and the inconvenient reality that much of contemporary conflict is irregular in character. Today in war, the consequential costs of failure, even of some success, tend to be higher than they were in the 20th century. It should be needless to say that the cost of failure in a major traditional war has always been high.

Since it would seem that the costs of war have risen while the potential rewards have fallen, it is not a hard sell or a leap of faith to claim that the utility of military force is on a sharp decline. Unfortunately, the foregoing would not be a safe judgment to make, as is said sometimes about legal verdicts. Plausible, perhaps not implausible, yes; true, probably not. Most especially is the judgment on the disutility of military force unsafe with regard to the possible behavior of noticeably un-American polities and societies (and tribes and gangs). Paradoxically, the very fact of war's obvious unattractiveness to America, and its closer friends and allies, must prove an incentive to America's enemies to fight on—and on.[14] This assertion seeks to oblige some contemporary noble hopes that masquerade as enlightened assumptions, to confront the enduring conflictive nature of our history. The spoils of victory are not what they once were—for example, territory, gold and other natural resources, and glory—but they are still substantial. The currencies of relative gain alter, but not the competition or the reality of winners and losers.

2. Times change — history is chronological, but it is not reliably linear.

To know the first decade of the 21st century is not to know the second or, indeed, any decade in the future. Some of the pathologies that typically are discernible in defense planning are confidently attributable to unsound approaches to genuine dilemmas. In truth there is no thoroughly sound way in which to prepare against the security and defense problems of tomorrow. Unfortunately, we have to attempt the impossible, which is why one should be empathetic towards those who must provide answers for questions that, as yet, are unspecified.[15] It is commonplace to refer to defense planning without being specific as to just what one means. For the purposes of this monograph, such planning is understood broadly rather than narrowly. Defense planning is approached here as any behavior that purposefully connects ends, ways, and means, and which pertains to the actual or conditionally possible use of military force. The plans can be regarded as strategies, and they may be more or less formal.[16] All too obviously the merit in our strategies, including our military plans, will depend upon their relevance to future circumstances, as well as to their performance when executed by our assets existing on the day of commitment.

Because of America's generally defensive stance in support of a values-based world order that it has had a considerable share in designing, plans and planning are apt to be a less useful way of coping with the future than one might suppose. In order to be as ready as it is able to cope with a future that it cannot design, America needs to prepare rather than plan. The planning function certainly is critically important, and it requires military professionals who are both educated in strategy and trained in how to produce plans. But it should be understood that beyond the revealed needs of today, the defense planner is engaged in defense preparation. And that preparation pertains to the ability to adapt well enough to the policy demands that arise out of contexts currently impossible to predict with high assurance.

The beginning of a prudent wisdom regarding the utility of military force is to recognize two inconvenient historical realities. First, times change. Moreover, times change frequently and unpredictably. Second, while our tiny temporal island of "today" necessarily looms largest in our relative significance rating for historical moments, such elevation of the present is always likely to mislead. Today must matter most, in the obvious sense that whatever the future holds has to flow from what is current. However, because we can only *attempt* to reset the future from today, it does not follow that we can be assured of success. It can be difficult even for historically educated people to appreciate realities that they find unwelcome. To be specific, people tend to resist the following plausible propositions:

- The notion of progress is a matter of definition; it carries particular meanings in particular cultures.
- Material advance and moral progress frequently are conflated and confused. Societies that become better equipped are not, *ipso facto*, better.
- Similarly, to be better off, in the sense of more wealthy, is not necessarily to be better in any way other than the material; indeed, increase in wealth may correlate with greater selfishness and a greater vulnerability as one's assets become more attractive to predators.

- Change need not mean progress.
- Change need not be linear and unidirectional.

Our judgment can hardly help being influenced by our values, and those will vary with time, place, and circumstance (see Proposition 3). It is only human to seek improvement, *inter alia,* and also it is human to confuse aspiration with probability. Our goal here is not the relatively easy one of identifying, understanding, and then explaining the contemporary balance of costs and benefits attendant upon the threat or use of military force. Even that duty is more complex than it may appear, because of the need to recognize variety (for example, of actor and strategic context). The challenge here is not to interpret the evidence of today for today. Instead, in effect it is to consider what, if anything, our current context means for the future. While today is most obviously a milestone on history's journey and has to be the departure gate for the remainder of the century, can it speak powerfully to the probable character of the strategic future?

Major plausible fallacies must be identified as such and duly need to be slain. First, there is the assumption that because today is different from the past, the latter is of no enduring consequence. The solemn, even banal, pronouncement that "times have changed," can be deployed portentously as the basis for the master claim that reference to old ideas and happenings as claimed analogies, is simply anachronistic.[17] Second, almost any historical self-awareness should advise that the future is not foreseeable and is not capable of being shaped and directed purposefully, and that it need not be characterized by features that suggest moral improvement. Because of the interplay of complexity, paradox, and irony, as noted earlier, it would be unwise to assume that the first decade of the 21st century tells us much that is useful about the whole of the century yet to come. Also, it would be imprudent to assume that this century must proceed in a generally linear fashion on a course extrapolated from the present and most recent past.

It is plausible to stake the claim for the 21st century that "this time it will be different" with respect to the nature of strategic history. When one draws inferences concerning the future from how bloody and unpredictable the 20th century was, one is often accused of anachronistic thinking. Because everything that occurs can happen only as a consequence of what went before, it is no simple matter to evade the snares of determinism. Given that few events are truly random even though caused, often it is difficult to argue persuasively on behalf of genuinely alternative futures. One suspects that the burden of *ex post facto* knowledge often is fatal for suitably capacious historical judgment. It can be said that the knowledge of what happened is a curse that the past puts on the historian who strives in vain to be properly elastic in his thinking, despite his unavoidable grasp of the consequences of decisions.

At this early juncture, I am suggesting what should be an unremarkable thesis: that we do not know what the 21st century will bring. This argument is best appreciated when we recognize that our predecessors did not know what their future would be, and we have no convincing reason to suppose that our future is any more reliably predictable than was theirs. If my argument is held to be plausible, even if contestable, it should at the very least suggest to readers that contemporary predictions anticipating the utility or disutility of military force in the future are not to be trusted.

3. The utility of military force varies with culture and circumstance.

Over-simple theory has a mighty ability to mislead. The simple idea that seems to capture and discipline a messy and therefore potentially uncontrollable reality all too often is simply wrong. Even more dangerous is the idea that is sound when applied adaptively with high contextual specificity, but almost begs to be misused. Two would-be imperial concepts lie at the core of this inquiry: the idea that military force has a utility, and the recent popularity of the more than marginally problematic idea of strategic culture.[18] These two ideas are central to the contemporary debate over the challenge to the kind of world order that is most favored and is substantially policed by the threat and use of American-led military power.

Before critics dash to their computers to complain that this author has long argued in praise of both military force as a potent instrument for order, and also for the importance of culture—most especially in the form of strategic culture—allow me to clarify. An essential concept should not be condemned or retired just because it is frequently misused. When adopted uncritically and without noticeably perceptive situational awareness, nearly every idea in the strategist's conceptual arsenal can be dangerous. Deterrence, arms control, irregular warfare, and peace, *inter alia*, are all perilous to adopt without discrimination. We shall return to the subject of strategic culture in the pages to follow.

The other idea that resides at the heart of this monograph is the proposition that force has utility, or should it be "a" utility? By addressing the subject of the utility of military force in the 21st century, the discussion may appear to concede preemptively that which really needs to be regarded as problematic. As phrased, the proposition certainly implies, I believe unsoundly, that military force has "[a?] utility as an instrument of policy." Sometimes, the quality of an answer is critically dependent on the sense in the question. But in this particular case, an implicit question poorly articulated does serve agreeably to elicit a meaningful answer. In fact, the problematic aspects of the term "utility of force," those that might attract scholarly criticism (utility to whom, where, when, and of what kinds?), act as a magnet for analysis that should be stimulating to clarity of thought about policy, strategy, and military tactics.

Despite the popularity and essential integrity of the idea that military force has utility for policy, qualities reinforced by General Sir Rupert Smith's important work on the subject, *The Utility of Force* (2005), the concept should always be accompanied by a notice advising "handle with care."[19] Why? The reasons for particularly careful handling include the following:

- Military force is not a simple quality/quantity that can be thoughts of and treated as an elementary particle, irreducible in substance; it is complex and comes in packages of differing sizes and contents.
- Warfare can take many forms — most obviously irregular, hybrid, regular, and something different with weapons of mass destruction (WMD).
- The utility of military force cannot depend only upon the quality and quantity of force threatened or applied, but most crucially upon the political determinant of required strategic effectiveness.

- One size will not fit all. Notwithstanding the many features of globalization that have the potential to smooth out some differences among still distinctive polities and their societies, the strategic contexts and cultures of actual and potential belligerents assuredly will be more or less asymmetrical.
- Even if, miraculously and improbably, one size in utility/disutility of military force were to fit nearly all polities, how much would that strange cultural fact matter, if and when their strategic circumstances were to vary hugely?
- Finally, on this very short list of skeptical thoughts, even if one were to sign on to the heroically commanding belief that the degree of the utility of military force can, as it were, be quantified over time, would one then be willing to claim that there is an unalterable trend showing the less military force applied, the better?

Still, we must be careful. Plainly, the subject of the utility of military force is of the highest importance. In addition, there is no doubt that what can be called the terms for its engagement as an active instrument of policy have changed; indeed, they have been changing for a long time. Recent realities of global communication and post-Cold War circumstances have encouraged the notion that "the sky is falling," all is changing. This is not entirely a foolish misperception. Times are changing. But the quintessential strategist's question, "So what?" can be augmented by another one, "When did they not?" It is necessary to come to grips with the cultural and situational dimensions that are vital to the sense in our examination, yet which frequently are not considered with sufficient rigor.

4. "Hard times make for soft principles."

We return now to the subject of strategic context and culture. It may be argued that strategic context is what you can make of it, while what you can make of it will be influenced strongly by what you bring to the task culturally. For an alternative and noticeably contrasting argument, you may argue that strategic culture is what you choose and are able to do in strategic circumstances that are both somewhat given, as well as negotiated competitively by threat and by the use of force, or by some positive inducement. The first definition suggests a rather fixed relationship between an objective strategic context and a no less objective strategic culture. The fourth proposition set forth above claims that "soft principles," or permissive culture, as a guide for action correlates with and results from stressful circumstances. The claim obviously empowers situation over culture in deciding between hard and soft principles.[20]

This theorist is unwilling to jump ship from the strategic cultural vessel on which he has been sailing for many years, but he is willing to move on from a view of the subject that may have been unduly static and insufficiently open to recognition of the potency of situation, contingency, and the universal nature of the individual human factor. In historical practice, contexts for the use of force tend by no means to be entirely "givens" for policymakers and soldiers. Proposition 4 makes the claim that people are likely to do what they believe they must do in order to succeed, perhaps just to survive, in the circumstances in which they find themselves. If embraced with undue enthusiasm, this assertion-prediction amounts to the claim that all is permissible under the lash of perceived necessity. From a historical perspective, it should be immediately apparent that this claim is seriously misleading. To be specific: most security communities are able to choose whether or not to use force, even in self-defense; similarly, when at war, most communities are able to exercise some discretion as to how much effort, and of what kinds, they will expend in the struggle. Of course, the enemy has a vote, "friction" happens,[21] contingency is active, and the course of the warfare will be a bloodily contested path negotiated by the competition in violence. However, polities are not puppets. And it makes no sense to discuss the utility of force as a great abstraction utterly innocent of reference to strategy.

Moral restraint on the style and quantity of war-making is a dimension — indeed, it can be an enabler — of strategy, though it is helpful to think of the relationship as being one of interdependence. Moral restraint works to limit ferocity, and it thereby enables force to be employed to advantage for political purposes.[22] Applied ethics, which is to say morality, is a necessary gatekeeper against the danger of "absolute war."[23] In the absence of such restraint, the nature of war is such that reciprocal ferocity is apt to produce an outcome of mutual ruination. The utility of force is a dependent variable governed primarily by political calculation. Whether or not the threat and use of force has utility depends not only on the character of the military force available, but rather more on the character of the political objectives to be pursued. However, even if the conflict in question is believed to be about political survival, and not merely advantage and disadvantage, it is by no means always the case that it is deemed sensible to exert all the force available. Restraint may be minimal, but still it is rare indeed for it to be absent altogether. History does not record many true wars of annihilation, wherein even genocide of the literal kind is found acceptable and possibly desirable. Such war is not entirely unknown, but it and its closer relatives in mass atrocity are outlier happenings, not routine episodes. The principal reason why this is so is not exactly mysterious — it is self-interest.[24] Warfare waged ferociously is apt to stimulate the enemy to behave likewise.

There is little doubt that there is some sense in the fourth preposition. Under the duress of war, polities do authorize their sword arms to behave in ways that are deemed legitimate and legal. Necessity is the excuse and the explanation; at least it is at present. Moreover, the UN Charter that now is the principal source of legal authority for the conduct of war, both recognizes self-defense as the inherent right of states and neglects to oblige them to receive the first blow. In international law, on many aspects the right to fight is notably discretionary.[25]

Notwithstanding the existence of a formidable body of laws, rules, norms, and customs that have been conflated by scholars into the compound concept of the "war convention," the fact remains that political behavior regarding the use of force is governed far more by considerations of prudent self-interest than it is by legal or ethical codes.[26] Fortunately, such codes for restraint that now are extant generally function to serve the interests of belligerents. But this fact should not be permitted to obscure another fact, which is that when polities experience crisis and wage war, they contend for the right to determine the rules of engagement (ROE) that best suit them. This is a variant on Thomas Schelling's famous description of warfare as a "diplomacy of violence," wherein the belligerents strive coercively to dominate the rules of the road for a particular conflict.[27]

To return to the main theme, it would be erroneous to postulate that either the times or one's principles must have some self-evident immanent quality (for example, the effect of hard times) that allow little discretion in action. Both times and principles will be givens for policymakers and soldiers, but scarcely ever is that the end of the story. Policy choice is straightforward, even if the options are all more or less unappealing, while principles typically require and allow for some interpretation. The cultural complexion of a society is not fixed, nor does it forbid exceptional behavior that may become blessed as authoritative precedent, even if it was first chosen in desperation out of a perceived brutal necessity. If a nation is behaving strategically, which in theory is the norm in human affairs, the utility of force is determined by what amounts to a negotiation between political ends and military means, mediated by the ways of strategy. Political ends reign and sometimes rule over ways and their means, but such authority is limited. Because military force is apt to be exceptionally costly when compared with the employment of the other grand-strategic instruments of policy, typically today its use requires an unusually strong justification.

However, to record this reality is not to argue that such force has lost utility, and still less is it to suggest that military force is yesterday's policy weapon. Nonetheless, it is valid to argue that the use of force is more costly today than was the case in the past. Ironically, the declining domain of the legitimacy of military force, and the diminishing discretion accorded over style of military use, render force particularly attractive to some belligerents. As political theater, expressive violence as a form of military force has no obviously superior rivals. Americans should not be surprised by the large measure of plausibility in this proposition. History, including contemporary history, shows that ethics are notably situational.[28] This is an unhappy reflection on our species, but it is one that is difficult to oppose convincingly. If we are sufficiently desperate, or angry and vengeful, we are probably capable of just about any character of nastiness. The proposition that military force has lost much of its utility is, alas, persuasive only with reference to a historical context wherein the perceived necessity for its large-scale employment is low and believed to be trending ever lower. As of this moment, there are no thoroughly compelling reasons to believe that "hard times" are now definitively ended, or that much harder times may well lie in the not far distant future. Once this claim is granted a serious audience, the fragility and imprudence of the argument for the decreasing utility of military force is revealed. The emperor is conceptually naked.

5. Warfare may be strategic surgery conducted under law for political ends, but also it is brute force or violence.

War is a legal condition that is defined most particularly by the fact that its motivation must be political. But it has the phenomenon of organized violence as a defining characteristic. Strictly speaking, force is made manifest in immediate consequence as violence. Force falls a little way short of being a euphemism for violence; admittedly, there is some daylight in meaning between the two terms. However, official references to violence done by our soldiers are eschewed by and large for reasons far removed from a commitment to clarity in the use of language. Liberal democracies today are not comfortable employing the inherently illiberal means that reside ready for use in the basket of options latent in military capabilities. There is tension between the high purposes frequently expressed in terms of values, and the low means by which they sometimes have to be advanced. This tension is revealed in the complexity of key relationships that lurk within the compound concept of the contemporary world order. This grand concept is a conflation of the following dimensions:

- Political order
- Legal order
- Social-cultural and moral order
- Military strategic order.

The discussion here pertains to the order of the social scientist, not the physical scientist. Everything impacts on everything else. As states rise and fall, they tend to provoke considerable disorder. In fact, it is necessary to recognize that world order, like culture, is ever in motion; it is always becoming something somewhat different. World order should be understood in the terms comparable to those with which Sheila Jager explains culture, namely, as "an on-going process of negotiation between past and present."[29] This "negotiation" can involve the "diplomacy of violence," to borrow again from Schelling. But liberal democracies today — and even yesterday — have difficulty understanding that the dynamism and complex processes of world order require support by the threat and occasional use of military force.

The black heart of the dilemma driving this discussion is the sheer nastiness of warfare (unpleasantness is far too mild a word). The dilemma that good people sometimes need to be ready and able to resort to bad means is typically resolved in one or both of two ways. One is that the military tools of violence are washed clean enough by the legitimate and virtuous purposes for which they are applied. The other is that the evil of the death and destruction wrought by military force is mitigated by a variety of means — technical, tactical, operational, strategic, legal, ethical, and political.

There are problems great and small with both of the approaches just cited for the laundering of war and warfare. A major difficulty with the long-standing and worthy endeavor to provide a hedge of technical restraints on war through variants upon the theme of "just war," is that the endeavor legitimizes, as well as constrains, the right to fight. Moreover, efforts to make the challenge of war an ethical matter and a legal one are ultimately doomed to failure. The reason should not be too difficult to grasp. Wars are not about ethics or law. This is not to deny that ethical traditions and a moral dimension, as well as legal argument, are relevant to public discourse and hence can have political and strategic implications. The point is that war is not fundamentally an ethical or a legal phenomenon despite the powerful influence that moral and legal arguments can have, especially in *post facto* debate. Individuals, organized groups, societies, politics, nations, and states always operate with mixed motivations. There are few, if any, causes for which there is and can be no justification, at least in some minds. True, there is some sense in the concepts of a common humanity, of people everywhere constituting a moral community, and of a universal international law. However, our enthusiasm for these noble ideals needs to be disciplined by recognition of the severe practical limits on their effective domain. And the problem lies not only in the frequency with which these grand conceptions are honored in the breach, but rather in the fact that each of them lends itself to contestable interpretation and hence exploitation as claimed justification for misdeeds. To make the matter plain beyond doubt, I am suggesting that international law provides a hunting license for those who wish to shoot, while moral argument is apt to be inherently contestable.[30]

If law and ethics are weak reeds to lean upon in taming military force (or violence), what can be said of technology, tactics, and strategy? Is it possible to civilize warfare, to wage war without the death and destruction imposed in warfare? The answer is no. However, warfare produces a spectrum of pain ranging from the precise and probably very sharp, all the way to blunt mega-economy size. The citizen as practicing ethicist has to ask himself whether quantity affects quality, in moral terms? Is military force more usable when it is applied carefully, in small measured amounts against objectively guilty targets? Whether military force is useful, as well as usable, is another matter, albeit a connected one. Plainly, military force has little utility if it is judged unusable on moral, legal, or political, grounds. In such circumstances, military force effectively is removed from the table of available options for grand strategy, meaning that its deterrent, preventive, and denial potential will be forfeit.

A problem, probably the problem, with technical, tactical, and strategic bundles of efforts to render warfare more acceptable to the liberal conscience, is that they must fail.[31] As the violent events of this century's early years remind us, even in an era when military force can be employed with unparalleled precision and calibration, force still manifests as violence that does damage and causes pain and death. One might have hoped that when America came to wage war with only regular volunteer soldiers, and to fight in the kinds of conflicts and in ways such that casualties would be unprecedentedly low by national historical standards, military force would be inoculated against serious ethical or political challenge. I must hasten to add, however, that the use of military force nearly always will be challengeable on political or strategic grounds. However, one might have expected a military instrument comprising only military professionals and applying force with high discrimination and discretion to be a readily usable and fairly noncontroversial tool of policy. Such has not proved to be the case.

It is of political and arguably of moral significance that military force can deliver a more precise blow than ever before. But in public discourse on military force, the noun is apt to trump the adjective. The bar is now much higher for acceptable instrumental violence. However, the issue here being social science and not physical science, one must acknowledge the strong probability that the moral judgment involved here is heavily situational, politically and strategically speaking. When Chancellor Otto von Bismarck observed that the Balkans were not worth the bones of a single Pomeranian grenadier, he flagged most helpfully the point that I must emphasize, namely, the intimate relationship between costs and expected gains. The utility of military force does not have a fixed-determinant value for a polity in a particular historical period. Rather, that utility must be estimated, meaning guessed, in particular cases at particular times — and one answer will not serve for all occasions.

Clausewitz warned against the perils of mistaking the character of a war for something that it is not, or trying to transform war into something that is alien to its nature.[32] It is in the nature of war to be violent. A military instrument may be capable of precise employment, but it remains a military instrument whose function is violence, notwithstanding the purposes for which it may be committed. The attendant political intentions are to be realized by military achievement.[33] Many scholars and other commentators have made the serious taxonomic error of inadvertently, innocently, treating war (and warfare) as though it were a branch of ethics or law. Their worthy efforts thus to tame war continue to be frustrated because the mission literally is impossible. Warfare as applied ethics or as "lawfare" inevitably is an illusion because it is in the DNA of war, as it were, to be political. The more thoroughgoing projects aimed at controlling and perhaps even eliminating war by means of ethical and legal restraints, choose to ignore the enduring reality that politics is the engine of war. In practice, warfare can escape political control and truly assume a purpose that is almost wholly self-regarding and autonomous. Although such a pathology is a real danger, however, it cannot threaten the normative point that warfare ought to be governed by politics, rather than vice versa. Effective legal restraint on war requires that there be a prior moral community, while the necessary moral community can exist and function as such only on the foundation of a notable measure of political community.[34] Military force has utility for reasons that ultimately are political by definition. Thus the logic of war matters more than does the grammar of war, though the latter is always of significance, since by definition it must entail threat, death and damage.[35]

6. Soft power substantially is not discretionary and the concept is more likely to mislead than to enlighten.

Soft power is a heroically imprecise concept, save only with respect to what it is not—hard power. If hard power is defined as the ability purposefully to inflict pain or to reward in the pursuit of influence, it is convenient and plausible to identify it with military and economic instruments of policy. Therefore, its opposite, soft power, is the ability to achieve influence by means other than military and economic. Joseph S. Nye, Jr., has been the principal spokesman for soft power. He explains as follows:

> Everyone is familiar with hard power. We know that military and economic might often get others to change their position. Hard power can rest on inducement ("carrots") or threats ("sticks"). But sometimes you can get the outcomes you want without tangible threats or payoffs. The indirect way to get what you want has sometimes been called "the second face of power." A country may obtain the outcomes it wants in world politics because other countries—admiring its values, emulating its example, aspiring to its level of prosperity and openness—want to follow it. In this sense, it is also important to set the agenda and attract others in world politics, and not only to force them to change by threatening military force or economic sanctions. This soft power—getting others to want the outcomes that you want—co-opts people rather than coerces them.[36]

Nye did not discover the seemingly glittering gem that is the idea of soft power, and he makes no attempt to suggest otherwise. We can say that he was the first to present the idea in full analytical rigor. Soft power has been enjoyed and exercised from the very beginning of human social interaction. The concept attracts attention today largely because it appears to offer an approach to the achievement of influence in world affairs that is complementary, and possibly even alternative, to that exercised through hard military and economic power.

Before proceeding further, it is essential to grasp the particular issue that we must regard as the examination question for this monograph. Specifically, the question is whether or not soft power can and should substitute for hard power. Further, if some substitution is possible, what are likely to be the advantages and disadvantages of each course, that is, of the United States achieving influence either "softly" or by means of the pain and reward of hard-tempered power? Let us explore the proposition that there is, or could be, a soft power substitute for hard military power. Whether or not military power retains an absolute utility, it may be determined that soft power can be as useful, or more so, and probably at only a fraction of the cost. In such comparisons, it is important not to be captured analytically by the posing of unhelpful mutual exclusives: soft power *or* hard power; utility *or* disutility; success *or* failure.

Soft power is potentially a dangerous idea not because it is unsound, which it is not, but rather for the faulty inference that careless or unwary observers draw from it. Such inferences are a challenge to theorists because they are unable to control the ways in which their ideas will be interpreted and applied in practice by those unwary observers. Concepts can be tricky. They seem to make sense of what otherwise is intellectually undergoverned space, and thus potentially come to control pliable minds. Given that men behave as their minds suggest and command, it is easy to understand why Clausewitz identified the enemy's will as the target for influence.[37] Beliefs about soft power in turn have potentially negative implications for attitudes toward the hard power of military force and economic muscle.

Thus, soft power does not lend itself to careful regulation, adjustment, and calibration. What does this mean? To begin with a vital contrast: whereas military force and economic pressure (negative or positive) can be applied by choice as to quantity and quality, soft power cannot. (Of course, the enemy/rival too has a vote on the outcome, regardless of the texture of the power applied.) But hard power allows *us* to decide how we will play in shaping and modulating the relevant narrative, even though the course of history must be an interactive one once the engagement is joined. In principle, we can turn the tap on or off at our discretion. The reality is apt to be somewhat different because, as noted above, the enemy, contingency, and friction will intervene. But still a noteworthy measure of initiative derives from the threat and use of military force and economic power. But soft power is very different indeed as an instrument of policy. In fact, I am tempted to challenge the proposition that soft power can even be regarded as one (or more) among the grand strategic instruments of policy.

The seeming validity and attractiveness of soft power lead to easy exaggeration of its potency. Soft power is admitted by all to defy metric analysis, but this is not a fatal weakness. Indeed, the instruments of hard power that do lend themselves readily to metric assessment can also be unjustifiably seductive. But the metrics of tactical calculation need not be strategically revealing. It is important to win battles, but victory in war is a considerably different matter than the simple accumulation of tactical successes. Thus, the burden of proof remains on soft power: (1) What is this concept of soft power? (2) Where does it come from and who or what controls it? and (3) Prudently assessed and anticipated, what is the quantity and quality of its potential influence? Let us now consider answers to these questions.

7. Soft power lends itself too easily to mischaracterization as the (generally unavailable) alternative to military and economic power.

The first of the three questions posed above all but invites a misleading answer. Nye plausibly offers the co-option of people rather than their coercion as the defining principle of soft power.[38] The source of possible misunderstanding is the fact that merely by conjuring an alternative species of power, an obvious but unjustified sense of equivalence between the binary elements is produced. Moreover, such an elementary shortlist implies a fitness for comparison, an impression that the two options are like-for-like in their consequences, though not in their methods. By conceptually corralling a country's potentially attractive co-optive assets under the umbrella of soft power, one is near certain to devalue the significance of an enabling context. Power of all kinds depends upon context for its value, but especially so for the soft variety. For power to be influential, those who are to be influenced have a decisive vote. But the effects of contemporary warfare do not allow recipients the luxury of a vote. They are coerced. On the other hand, the willingness to be co-opted by American soft power varies hugely among recipients. In fact, there are many contexts wherein the total of American soft power would add up in the negative, not the positive. When soft power capabilities are strong in their values and cultural trappings, there is always the danger that they will incite resentment, hostility, and a potent "blowback." In those cases, American soft power would indeed be strong, but in a counterproductive direction. These conclusions imply no criticism of American soft power *per se*. The problem would lie in the belief that soft power is a reliable instrument of policy that could complement or in some instances replace military force.

8. Soft power is perilously reliant on the calculations and feelings of frequently undermotivated foreigners.

The second question above asked about the provenance and ownership of soft power. Nye correctly notes that "soft power does not belong to the government in the same degree that hard power does." He proceeds sensibly to contrast the armed forces along with plainly national economic assets with the "soft power resources [that] are separate from American government and only partly responsive to its purposes."[39] Nye cites as a prominent example of this disjunction in responsiveness the fact that "[i]n the Vietnam era . . . American government policy and popular culture worked at cross-purposes."[40] Although soft power can be employed purposefully as an instrument of national policy, such power is notably unpredictable in its potential influence, producing net benefit or harm. Bluntly stated, America is what it is, and there are many in the world who do not like what it is. The U.S. Government will have the ability to project American values in the hope, if not quite confident expectation, that "the American way" will be found attractive in alien parts of the world. Our hopes would seem to be achievement of the following: (1) love and respect of American ideals and artifacts (civilization); (2) love and respect of America; and (3) willingness to cooperate with American policy today and tomorrow. Admittedly, this agenda is reductionist, but the cause and desired effects are accurate enough. Culture is as culture does and speaks and produces. The soft power of values culturally expressed that others might find attractive is always at risk to negation by the evidence of national deeds that appear to contradict our cultural persona.

Moreover, no contemporary U.S. government owns all of America's soft power—a considerable understatement. Nor do contemporary Americans and their institutions own all of their country's soft power. America today is the product of America's many yesterdays, and the worldwide target audiences for American soft power respond to the whole of the America that they have perceived, including facts, legends, and myths.[41] Obviously, what they understand about America may well be substantially untrue, certainly it will be incomplete. At a minimum, foreigners must react to an American soft power that is filtered by their local cultural interpretation. America is a future-oriented country, ever remaking itself and believing that, with the grace of God, history moves forward progressively toward an ever-better tomorrow. This optimistic American futurism both contrasts with foreigners' cultural pessimism—their golden ages may lie in the past, not the future—which prevails in much of the world and is liable to mislead Americans as to the reception our soft power story will have.[42] Many people indeed, probably most people, in the world beyond the United States have a fairly settled view of America, American purposes, and Americans. This locally held view derives from their whole experience of exposure to things American as well as from the features of their own "cultural thoughtways" and history that shape their interpretation of American-authored words and deeds, past and present.[43]

This is not to say that soft power is unimportant or invariably misapprehended. Perceptions of America can and do alter over time. But the soft power of ideas and of practices that non-Americans may be persuaded to adopt and possibly adapt with consequences favorable for U.S. interests, do not constitute a policy instrument (or basket of such instruments) seriously comparable to military force. The greatest among history's great powers have usually been attractive civilizations worthy of admiration and emulation as well as potent coercers.[44] Many foreigners have desired to join the contemporary winner not only for reasons of crude self-interest, but also to share the hegemonic power's style of living and advanced thought. The flattery of imitation has an ancient historical lineage. Imperial rule as well as the less mandatory hegemonic influence has always been manifested in the practice of more or less voluntary co-option of those who deemed it prudent, advantageous, and generally sensible to "follow the leader."

All great powers should command respect, and not infrequently they are also feared. But few genuinely inspire a desire in others to emulate them culturally, save for reasons of anticipated material advantage. For example, China today does serve as a model worthy of respect for its thus far successful blending of economic advance with tight political control. However, such respect rests upon no normative element beyond the values of greed and political discipline (values refer only to that which is valued). The Chinese practice of governance might just possibly be an example of soft power, but to label it thus betrays democratic values. One could as well say that Benito Mussolini's Italy enjoyed some soft-power benefit as an example of strong anti-democratic rule. Indeed, the brutal modernist dictatorships of communism, fascism, and nazism, as well as their more or less pale reflections outside Europe, provided much evidence of soft power. Dictatorial leaders and party functionaries adopted and adapted foreign ideas of a firm hand both because they appeared to work well, and because the ideas of leadership, social discipline, and a congeries of repressive measures held quite genuine appeal. When Americans today think about the appeal of soft power, they often forget that the concept is content-free. It is about voluntary co-option for reason of an attraction of values, but it says nothing about the particular values that are borrowed and somewhat nationalized. A liking for genocide of the "unworthy" has been known to have appeal across political and cultural frontiers. Soft power is not by definition only the soft power of humane liberal values.

It bears repeating because it passes unnoticed that culture, and indeed civilization itself, are dynamic, not static phenomena. They are what they are for good and sufficient local geographical and historical reasons, and cannot easily be adapted to fit changing political and strategic needs. For an obvious example, the dominant American strategic culture, though allowing exceptions, still retains its principal features, the exploitation of technology and mass.[45] These features can be pathological when circumstances are not narrowly conducive to their exploitation. Much as it was feared only a very few years ago that, in reaction to the neglect of culture for decades previously, the cultural turn in strategic studies was too sharp, so today there is a danger that the critique of strategic culturalism is proceeding too far.[46] The error lies in the search for, and inevitable finding of, "golden keys" and "silver bullets" to resolve current versions of enduring problems. Soft-power salesmen have a potent product-mix to sell, but they fail to appreciate the reality that American soft power is a product essentially unalterable over a short span of years. As a country with a cultural or civilizational brand that is unique and mainly rooted in deep historical, geographical, and ideational roots, America is not at liberty to emulate a major car manufacturer and advertise an extensive and varied model range of persuasive soft-power profiles. Of course, some elements of soft power can be emphasized purposefully in tailored word and deed. However, foreign perceptions of the United States are no more developed from a blank page than the American past can be retooled and fine-tuned for contemporary advantage. Frustrating though it may be, a country cannot easily escape legacies from its past.

9. The domain for the policy utility of soft power typically is either structurally permissive of easy success, or is unduly resistant to such influence.

The third fundamental question about soft power in need of answer can best be posed in only two words, "So what?" The combined fallacies of misnaming and over-simplification that threaten the integrity and utility of the concept of soft power are more than merely an academic itch that can be scratched into oblivion. The soft power concept is sufficiently valid intellectually that its contestable evidential base in history and thus its true fragility are easily missed. To explain its logic: soft power resides in the ability to co-opt the willing rather than to coerce or compel the reluctant; American soft power attracts non-Americans because it represents or advances values, ideas, practices, and arrangements that they judge to be in their interest, or at least to which they feel some bond of affinity. Therefore, the soft power of the American hegemon is some conflation of perceived interests with ideological association (by and large more tacit than explicit).

Full-blown, the argument holds, first, that America (for example) gains useful political clout if and when foreigners who matter highly to U.S. national security share important American understandings, values, and preferences. The thesis proceeds in its second step to package this thus far commonsense proposition under the banner of "soft power"; it is now dangerously objectified, as if giving something a name causes it to exist. Next, the third and most problematic step in the argument is the logical leap that holds that American soft power, as existing reality—what it is, and its effects—can be approached and treated usefully as an instrument of national policy. This is an attractive proposition: it is unfortunate that its promise is thoroughly unreliable. The problem lies in the extensive middle region that lies between a near harmony of values and perceived interests and, at the opposite end of the spectrum, a close to complete antagonism between those values and interests. Historical evidence as well as reason suggest that the effective domain of soft power is modest. The scope and opportunity for co-option by soft power are even less. People and polities have not usually been moved far by argument, enticement, and attractiveness. There will be some attraction to, and imitation of, a great power's ideas and practical example, but this fact has little consequence for the utility of military force. Indeed, one suspects that on many occasions what might be claimed as a triumph for soft power is in reality no such thing. Societies and their political leaders may be genuinely attracted to some features of American ideology and practice, but the clinching reason for their agreement to sign on to an American position or initiative will be that the United States looks convincing as a guardian state and coalition leader.

It is not difficult to identify reasons why military force seems to be less useful as a source of security than it once was. But it is less evident that soft power can fill the space thus vacated by the military and economic tools of grand strategy. Soft power should become more potent, courtesy of the electronic revolution that enables a networked global community. The ideological, political, and strategic consequences of such globalization, however, are not quite as benign as one might have predicted. It transpires that Francis Fukuyama was wrong; the age of ideologically fueled hostility has not passed after all.[47] Also, it is not obvious that the future belongs to a distinctively Western civilization.[48] It is well not to forget that the Internet is content-blind, and it advertises, promotes, and helps enable bloody antagonism in addition to the harmony of worldview that many optimists have anticipated. It does not follow from all this that the hard power of military force retains, let alone increases, its utility as an instrument of policy. But assuredly it does follow that the historical motives behind defense preparation are not greatly diminished. Thus, there is some noteworthy disharmony between the need for hard power and its availability, beset as it increasingly is by liberal global attitudes that heavily favor restraint.

10. Hard and soft power should be complementary, but unless one is strategically competent, neither will have high utility for policy, either singly or "jointly."

An inherent and unavoidable problem with a country's soft power is that it is near certain to be misassessed by the politicians who attempt to govern soft power's societal owners and carriers. Few thoroughly encultured Americans are likely to undervalue "the American way" in many of its aspects as a potent source of friendly self-co-option abroad. Often, this self-flattering appreciation will be well justified in reality. But as an already existing instrument of American policy, the soft power of ideas and practical example is fraught with the perils of self-delusion. If one adheres to an ideology that is a heady mixture of Christian ethics ("one nation, under God . . ."), democratic principles, and free market orthodoxy, and if one is an American, which is to say if one is a citizen of a somewhat hegemonic world power that undeniably has enjoyed a notably successful historical passage to date, then it is natural to confuse the national ideology with a universal creed. Such confusion is only partial, but nonetheless it is sufficiently damaging as to be a danger to national strategy.

Since it is fallacious to assume that American values truly are universal, the domain of high relevance and scope for American soft power to be influential is distinctly limited. If one places major policy weight on the putative value for policy of American soft power, one needs to be acutely alert to the dangers of an under-recognized ethnocentrism born of cultural ignorance. This ignorance breeds an arrogant disdain for evidence of foreigners' lack of interest in being co-opted to join American civilization. The result of such arrogance predictably is political and even military strategic counterreaction. It is a case of good intentions gone bad when they are pursued with indifference toward the local cultural context.

Some people have difficulty grasping the unpalatable fact that much of the world is not receptive to any American soft power that attempts to woo it to the side of American interests. Not all rivalries are resolvable by ideas, formulas, or "deals" that seem fair and equitable to us. There are conflicts wherein the struggle is the message, to misquote Marshal MacLuhan, with value in the eyes of local belligerents. Not all local conflicts around the world are amenable to the calming effect of American soft power. True militarists of left and right, secular and religious, find intrinsic value in struggle and warfare, as A. J. Coates has explained all too clearly.

> The self-fulfilment and self-satisfaction that war generates derive in part from the religious or ideological significance attributed to it and from the resultant sense of participating in some grand design. It may be, however, that the experience of war comes to be prized for its own sake and not just for the great ends that it serves or promotes. For many, the excitement unique to war makes pacific pursuits seem insipid by comparison. This understanding and experience of moral, psychological, and emotional self-fulfillment increase our tolerance for war and threaten its moral regulation. It transforms war from an instrumental into an expressive activity.[49]

It is foolish to believe that every conflict contains the seeds of its own resolution, merely awaiting suitable watering through co-option by soft power. To be fair, similarly unreasonable faith in the disciplinary value of (American) military force is also to be deplored.

Returning to the role of strategy, if America is strategically incompetent, it will not matter much which, if any, policy instruments are available for execution. One must add the codicil that, for good or ill, it is easier to employ military force on behalf of policy than it is to attempt to tailor one's soft power to fit the exact need of the political moment. If military force is apt to be a blunt instrument that lends itself to producing unintended consequences, such indeterminacy of effects pales when compared to the problematic impact of the soft power lurking in American civilization. There is a monumental arrogance accompanied by a breathtaking optimism about the proposition that soft power should be an instrument of national policy. Of course, one cannot simply dismiss soft power because the historical evidence of its partial efficacy is undeniable. Soft power is not an illusion, but it is ever likely to be uncontrollable and hence to defy strategic employment. Effects-based planning for grand strategy must be so problematic with reference to soft power, with its uncertain reception, as to require a large policy-health warning.

As for the complementarity of hard and soft power, there are so many unknowable third- and fourth-order effects, such redundancy of feedback loops, and so much genuine indeterminacy of relative weights of causal effects that it is extremely difficult to proceed to an analytically satisfactory common-sense level of appreciation. Can we distinguish between voluntary co-option for reason of affection or respect, and co-option because of cynical calculation of material self-interest? It is not so much the values and beliefs of foreigners that matter, but rather their behavior. States cooperate with each other and sometimes tolerate inflicted harm, because they respect the ability and presume a willingness on the part of the villainous party to inflict yet greater damage. Values are apt to be found compatible with perceived necessity in the rough world of politics, domestic and international. The more authority that is accorded hard capabilities for influence, the greater the ease with which soft power works its salubrious wonders. Great powers have ever believed that they deserve some authority over their geographical neighborhood.[50] This belief has normative content; it is not merely descriptive of relative strength of ability to impose political will. The more "rightful" a great power's hegemony is deemed to be by its neighboring states and societies, the more influence one should expect of its apparently soft power. Authority accepted as legitimate and appropriate should be in scant need of military, economic, or other direct forms of enforcement.

However, the complementarity between hard and soft power that would seem to produce a regional hegemony is apt to fail in the face of the antagonism natural among human societies. Neighboring states, whether of equal or unequal standing in material assets for power, tend to be antagonists.[51] They have much more to fight about than do polities distant from each other, since both military and cultural menace is more proximate and severe. Those among us who are attracted by the idea of soft power, most especially when the concept is contrasted with military force, need to come to terms with the ferocity with which civil warfare tends to be prosecuted. The substantial currency of soft power that multiple communities in a single would-be polity share is in practice often overwhelmed by conflict-based ideational and economic differences. Americans who are strongly attracted to the appealing concept of soft power should reflect upon its applicability to their own civil war, the most bloody conflict in American history.

11. Soft power and hard power are more mutually enabling than they are fungible.

While it is sensible to seek influence abroad as cost-effectively as possible, it is only prudent to be modest in one's expectations of the soft power to be secured by cultural influence. There are few, if any, absolutes in this analysis, and the choices are not strictly either/or. Military and economic coercion is not reliable because the coercee is at liberty to decline to be coerced, albeit at a cost. But influence sought through the target's exposure to "the American way" is even less likely to lend itself to predictable effects-based grand-strategic planning. Every polity and society have features in which they take pride—and the sources of pride can vary widely in ways under-recognized abroad. The soft power of America in all its aspects is not entirely a power likely to produce American advantage. As with all other polities, the United States has exhibited a gap between noble collective aspiration and some ignoble behavior. Foreign audiences are guided in their interpretation of the American reality not by an objective standard, but rather through the filter of their own local culture. In other words, if one seeks to export the American way purposefully as a soft power instrument of national policy, one has to recall that Americans will not be able to control the images of the American civilizational message as they will be perceived abroad. This is not to say that there is no soft power, far from it. Instead, it is to say that such power is more like a wild card than a tool of known universal utility.

Sad to relate, there is no convincing evidence suggesting an absence of demand for the threat and use of military force. I write this in the context of prior acknowledgment of a still burgeoning "war convention" that places potential restraints on the use of force. But insecurity conditions continue to require the menace of military force for their alleviation and occasional resolution, even though the supply of such force at present is ever problematic. One should not be confused by the trend in a more globalized world toward restraining the military force that might be deployed by the agents of order. Military force is more costly to threaten and employ than it used to be, but it is not necessarily always less useful or usable. Indeed, the culture shock to liberal Westerners on witnessing the exercise of brute force, can have a political value for reason of its shocking political incorrectness. Consider the highly aggressive pre-planned use of military power by Russia against U.S.-leaning Georgia in 2008. For all the negative commentary that Moscow attracted from abroad, the net balance of consequences between costs and political rewards probably was significantly weighted in favor of the rewards. Although Russia gained respect for its political will by its aggressive behavior, the benefit was less than it might have been had the United States and its North Atlantic Treaty Organization (NATO) allies not been so actively engaged in their own military coercion during the Gulf wars.

Some readers might believe mistakenly that I demean or dismiss soft power. This is not so. True, the argument advanced here has found soft power to be a less useful tool of policy than is popularly supposed, but this finding falls a fair distance short of dismissal. Considering hard and soft power as partial or complete substitutes for each other, the following uncomfortable conclusions emerge:

- There are cases in which neither soft power nor hard power is able to deliver advantage, let alone victory. Moreover, it is probable that no combination of them could succeed. Scholars usually are able to postulate a miraculously effective hypothetical intervention in the sad course of history that should have delivered success, but such can only be idle speculation.
- Soft power is not a matter of either/or. It is entirely possible for much of American culture to be shared and respected, but for that fact to count for little with reference to policy choice. Societies can penetrate each other deeply with some of their values and practices, while simultaneously having a largely conflictual relationship for reason of interests perceived to be incompatible.
- Historically, a context of total mutual disrespect among antagonistic societies and polities is unusual. Politics and the interests that drive it have a way of suppressing much cultural admiration, let alone affinity. When national interests are perceived as clashing, soft power is an early victim. Examples abound, but prominent cases include the rise of Anglo-German antagonism from the late 19th century, and that of American-Japanese antagonism in the 20th century.[52]

- While soft power theory offers the agreeable proposition that American values and culture generally have some ability to co-opt "others" in an attractively economical way, historical evidence seems to point in a different direction. More accurately, the relationship is one wherein soft power flows to the owner of hard power. Thucydides in ca. 400 BC is to be recommended as a more reliable guide to international relations and foreign policy in the 21st century than is Joseph S. Nye.[53]
- Soft power is real and might often do some good around the edges of policy. But soft power is mainly fool's gold when it is considered as a bona fide instrument of (American) policy.
- But to question the efficacy of soft power is not, *ipso facto*, to praise the utility of military force. A challenge for policy in the 21st century reposes in the reality that neither hard nor soft power is a reliable policy tool. A key difference between the two, though, is that while it is both necessary and practicable to regard military force as a policy instrument, such cannot be claimed for soft power. Unlike American soft power, its military power is not an inherent given. The capability to threaten and use military power is highly variable, even contingent, and requires centralized official direction. Soft power is thoroughly different. It is diffuse, substantially "given" and unalterable by sudden central decision, and its effects (first, second, third order?) on particular foreign audiences are not easily predictable.

CONCLUSION

The discussion has ranged widely over topics both central and modestly tangential to the question of the utility of military force in the 21st century. Because this analysis has an educational rather than prescriptive purpose, the focus has been upon how to think about the relevance of military power as an instrument of policy — most especially in relation to soft power — as a substitute or complement. Five findings merit special notice. They contain at least implicit recommendations regarding the utility of military force. Practical applicability must, of course, be a function of actual historical context. However, the United States and its Army are more likely to make wise specific choices if they enjoy a secure understanding in general terms. General theory, meaning explanation, is essential education for the applied theory known as historical strategies and plans.[54]

1. Military force is not an anachronism; it is and will long remain an essential instrument of policy.

Military force is not discretionary as an item in the policy tool bag. Military force is not always the right tool to employ, and even when it is appropriate, there is no guarantee that it will be used effectively — but these are matters extrinsic to the main point. There are conflicts that cannot be resolved politically, sufficiently alleviated by diplomacy or any other nonmilitary means, or settled by some tolerable compromise. For reasons amply covered in Thucydides's triptych of "fear, honor, and interest," warfare is a necessary option as a sanction against unacceptable behavior by hostile polities and other belligerents.[55] The fact that

it often does not deliver a politically satisfactory outcome is beside the point. Medicine and surgery do not
always work as required, either. Public opinion in a
notably pacifist liberal West tends to favor the attitude
that military force is anachronistic. The use of force
is usually held to be evidence of policy failure, since
wiser policy should have succeeded in prevention.
This view is as understandable as it is fashionable, but
still it is wrong. Even wise policy can fail, for example,
when foreign political leaders decline to be deterred
despite the obvious dictates of reason. Just as military
force has a unique ability among policy tools to create
expensive havoc, so also it has a distinctive capacity to
enable favorable decisions. The fact that military force
should be used only with great care and skill does not
minimize its unique importance. Warfare has shaped
and reshaped the course of history more significantly
than has any other impulse in the whole human experience.[56]

**2. Military force is not under threat of obsolescence
because of the availability of "smart" soft power
alternatives, but its utility to liberal Western societies is menaced by the imprudent measure of their
imprudent enthusiasm for placing constraints upon
their use of it.**

This second finding should not be taken as evidence of a reckless gung-ho attitude toward the threat
and use of military force. My concern is that our contemporary determination to employ force justly and
decently is in some danger of imperiling the prospects
for success in military missions. Of course, military
force should be used only as necessary and in the
quantity suitable to its task. The problem today is that

our Western societies are more than a little ambivalent about the official use of force. Since military force as an option in the policy tool bag is mandatory for public safety, order, and prosperity, the challenge to politicians and educated commentators is two-fold. On the one hand, it is essential that our military force is applied in accordance with reasonable interpretation of "just war" principles. But on the other, it is also necessary that our authoritative legal and political interpretations of those principles do not destroy our ability to prevail militarily when we must.[57] If we are not really convinced that we must prevail, then we ought not to be fighting. The man in the street, qua strategist, needs to understand that General William Tecumseh Sherman was correct—war is hell. Warfare without pain is an oxymoron.

3. Strategic competency is key to the utility of military force for policy, but is less relevant to soft power.

It is not quite valid to argue that strategy is the key to the utility of both hard military (and economic) power and of soft power. Whereas strategy should direct the military instrument according to the logic of ends, ways, and means, soft power by its nature does not lend itself to such control. American soft power is largely what it is, regardless of official ambitions for its effectiveness as a policy tool. The strategy function is not entirely irrelevant, in that soft power can be considered in the classic terms, just cited—ends, ways, and means. American military power is essentially a tamed force (disciplined violence), even though it may behave unpredictably in the interactive, dynamic, and friction-prone environment of war. The country's soft power, however, is notably untamed and untameable. Because hard power and soft power roll off the tongue as though they are comparable, even largely matching, concepts, they are in fact totally asymmetrical, with soft power on the short end. The two options are significantly beyond useful comparison. Hard power and soft power are indeed two species of the power genus. But the differences in all aspects of power generation between the two species render the mere act of comparing them itself misleading. From the perspective of public policy, military force is owned uniquely by legitimate central political authority, whereas most of the components of soft power are not grown, owned, or controllable at will by policymakers. If military force is akin to a domesticated animal, soft power is more like one that cannot be domesticated. Soft power is a dangerous concept, because it sounds far more usable than it is.

4. There is strategic advantage in moral advantage, which translates as a requirement for the use of military force to be plainly legitimate. [58]

To wage only just wars justly cannot guarantee success, but to wage unjust wars unjustly is close to a guarantee of failure in the 21st century. The relevant law and ethical precepts are clear enough, but they are so subject to local interpretation, even when sincerely undertaken, that the guidance they provide is a great deal less prescriptively useful than they appear to promise. Sadly, both law and ethics are found useful in practice in good part because they lend themselves to permissive self-serving justification by belligerents. That said, there is a moral dimension to international conflict,[59] albeit one that is severely short of objective and authoritative policing. Ethics are universal, but specific ethical philosophies, traditions, and schools vary hugely. Much of the universality of ethics disappears down the cracks created by particular cultures, local contexts, priorities, values, and habits. Since the human will is the most important component of fighting power, the readiness of that will to apply itself to the lethal business of warfare has to be a subject of prime strategic importance. We humans are moral beings, meaning that we are all more or less in thrall to one or more ethical tradition that educates, even programs, our moral judgment. Soldiers do not fight hard for a cause because that cause objectively is "just," but rather because they believe it to be so. If confidence in the rightness of a soldier's efforts is shaken, there are certain to be consequences adverse to his or her military effectiveness. The hard power of military force is especially vulnerable to enfeeblement by the ill consequences of moral self-doubt. Our liberal Western democracies are not warrior societies.[60] The values of militarism are not the ones that we endorse and encourage, even among our professional soldiers. However, in contrast to the European context in general, the United States does appear to encourage some attitudes in its military personnel that verge upon the militaristic. The frontier between militarism and military professionalism is crossed when prowess in warfare is regarded as a value in itself, as expressive achievement, rather than as an instrumental value. Properly explained, the behavior of American soldiers, including warriors (few soldiers truly are or need to be warriors),[61] is not "about" warfare; instead it is "about" the generation of strategic effects on behalf of the ends of political policy. Liberal Western societies need the services of some warriors — among the mass of its soldiers—who will deliver military force for reasons and in ways that they have no great difficulty understanding as legitimate. If the moral dimension to a contemporary conflict is devalued during the ongoing audit of public perception, then the nation's strategic effort is all but certain to be fatally damaged. There will be a spiral of self-doubt at home and in the field, characterized by diminished military effectiveness, encouragement of the enemy, and an inevitable search for guilty people to blame.

5. Soft power tends to co-opt the readily co-optable, while hard military power is necessary for more demanding missions.

Paradox and irony reign over strategic matters.[62] It is paradoxical that soft power works well when it is not needed, but is irrelevant or nearly so when it could make all the difference. America requires hard military and economic power, effectively guided by good enough strategy, precisely because the country's soft power does not enjoy universal dominion. A world of states, nations, and societies that is not immediately recognizable as being at least a simulacrum of the American model of culture and civilization cannot be regarded as an audience palpitating for enlightenment. This thought is heretical to many Americans who believe we as a nation are on a historical missionary journey for the general improvement of Mankind. The American civilization is heavily ideological. Indeed, the whole notion of soft power in its appeal to Americans resides in the linked beliefs that: (1) our way is the better way, and (2) understanding of our way on the part of "Others" will induce, or seduce, them into becoming co-optees to the American worldview. The basis of the high regard Americans are inclined to have for soft power—aside from its low cost as compared with military force—lies in cultural hubris. It seems rarely to occur to us that we ourselves might be more vulnerable to civilizational co-option than are some others. Nor are we sure whether our apparent co-opting of others by soft power is received with genuine appreciation or as a prudent calculation. Overall, although having soft power is always welcome, the contexts wherein its presumably benign effects would be most useful are precisely those where it is least likely to work its magic successfully.

ENDNOTES

1. Joseph S. Nye, Jr., *The Paradox of American Power: Why the World's Only Superpower Can't Go It Alone*, New York: Oxford University Press, 2002, p. 4.

2. Gavin Lyall, *Spy's Honour*, London, UK: Coronet Books, 1993, p. 51.

3. Clausewitz defines war as "an act of force to compel our enemy to do our will." Carl von Clausewitz, *On War*, Michael Howard and Peter Paret, eds. and trans., Princeton, NJ: Princeton University Press, 1976, p. 75 (emphasis in the original).

4. See Richard E. Neustadt and Ernest R. May, *Thinking in Time: The Uses of History for Decision-Makers*, New York: The Free Press, 1986; Williamson Murray and Richard Hart Sinnreich, eds., *The Past as Prologue: The Importance of History to the Military Profession Today*, New York: Cambridge University Press, 2006; Jeremy Black, *Rethinking Military History*, Abingdon, MA: Routledge, 2004; Jeremy Black, *The Curse of History*, London, UK: The Social Affairs Unit, 2008; and Margaret Macmillan, *The Uses and Abuses of History*, London, UK: Profile Books, 2009.

5. "Without a theory the facts are silent." F. A. Hayek, quoted in John Keegan, *A History of Warfare*, London, UK: Hutchinson, 1993, p. 6.

6. For years, possibly decades, I have poured scorn on the misleading concept of the "foreseeable future," but thus far, obviously in vain, given its continuing popularity. See Colin S. Gray, *Fighting Talk: Forty Maxims on War, Peace, and Strategy*, Westport, CT: Praeger Security International, 2007, pp. 155-157.

7. See Lawrence Freedman, *The Transformation of Strategic Affairs*, Adelphi Paper 378, London, UK: International Institute for Strategic Studies, March 2006.

8. Oliver Wendell Holmes, Jr., quoted in Robert J. McMahon, *Dean Acheson and the Creation of an American World Order*, Washington, DC: Potomac Books, 2009, p. 14.

9. Michael Ignatieff, *The Warrior's Honor: Ethnic War and the Modern Conscience*, London, UK: Chatto and Windus, 1998, p. 8.

10. See Rupert Smith, *The Utility of Force: The Art of War in the Modern World*, London, UK: Allen Lane, 2005.

11. David Kennedy, *Of War and Law*, Princeton, NJ: Princeton University Press, 2006, pp. 12, 125.

12. See A. J. Coates, *The Ethics of War*, Manchester, UK: Manchester University Press, 1997, Chap. 8.

13. Clausewitz, pp. 85-86.

14. To assert this is not to indulge in a crudely "realistic" essentialism. For a short selection from a large literature, see John A. Vasquez, *The Power of Power Politics: From Classical Realism to Neotraditionalism*, Cambridge, UK: Cambridge University Press, 1998; Jack Donnelly, *Realism and International Relations*, Cambridge, UK: Cambridge University Press, 2000; Jonathan Haslam, *Realist Thought in International Relations since Machiavelli*, New Haven, CT: Yale University Press, 2002; and Michael C. Williams, ed., *Realism Reconsidered: The Legacy of Hans J. Morgenthau in International Relations*, Oxford, UK: Oxford University Press, 2007.

15. See Colin S. Gray, "Strategic Thoughts for Defence Planners," *Survival*, Vol. 52, No. 3, June-July 2010, pp. 159-178, which might lend itself to the charge of a lack of empathy.

16. See Colin S. Gray, *The Strategy Bridge: Therory for Practice,* Oxford: Oxford University Press, 2010, for the full story.

17. To cite a personal example, I was informed recently by a very distinguished retired four-star general that the challenges of cyberspace are so novel that past experience is irrelevant. It was, and remains, my view that cyber power in any and all of its aspects is thoroughly comprehensible within the framework of the general theory of strategy (as are land power, sea power, air power, and space power). The need to understand the implications of new kinds of technology is an entirely familiar demand on our imagination. This is not to claim that cyberspace, let alone cyber warfare, is anything other than an intellectually undergoverned domain at present.

18. Especially useful studies include Lawrence Sondhaus, *Strategic Culture and Ways of War*, Abingdon, MA: Routledge, 2006; Jeannie L. Johnson, Kerry M. Kartchner, and Jeffrey A. Larsen, eds., *Strategic Culture and Weapons of Mass Destruction: Culturally Based Insights into Comparative National Security Policymaking*, New York: Palgrave Macmillan, 2009; and, for a strongly sceptical view, Patrick Porter, *Military Orientalism: Eastern War Through Western Eyes,* London, UK: C. Hurst, 2009.

19. Smith, *The Utility of Force.*

20. An essentialist approach to culture is critiqued robustly in Porter, *Military Orientalism.*

21. Clausewitz, pp. 119-121.

22. This logic is developed powerfully in Coates, *The Ethics of War;* Christopher Coker, *Ethics and War in the 21st Century*, Abingdon, MA: Routledge, 2008, is also relevant.

23. See Clausewitz, pp. 488-489, 579.

24. See Coker, *Ethics and War in the 21st Century*, p. 23.

25. This is the principal message in Kennedy, *Of War and Law.*

26. Michael Walzer, *Just and Unjust Wars: A Moral Argument with Historical Illustrations*, 3rd Ed., New York: Basic Books, 2000, Part 3.

27. Thomas C. Schelling, *Arms and Influence*, New Haven, CT: Yale University Press, 1966, Chap. 1.

28. See the discussion in Colin S. Gray, "Moral Advantage, Strategic Advantage?" *The Journal of Strategic Studies*, Vol. 33, No. 3, June 2010, pp. 333-365.

29. Sheila Miyoshi Jager, *On the Uses of Cultural Knowledge*, Carlisle, PA: Strategic Studies Institute, U.S. Army War College, November 2007, p. 9.

30. See Kennedy, *Of War and Law*, Chap. 3.

31. I am a little embarrassed to employ such a reductionist term as the liberal conscience, but it enjoys such distinguished endorsement and is so familiar that I choose to discount my reservations. See the classic treatment in Michael Howard, *War and the Liberal Conscience*, London, UK: Hurst Publishers, 2008.

32. Clausewitz, p. 88. The Prussian's insight is deep, though he did invite confusion with his rather flexible employment of the concept of the nature of war. I believe it is important to distinguish clearly and consistently between war's enduring nature and its ever-changing character. A somewhat more permissive view of the variability of war's nature is favored in Antulio J. Echevarria II, *Clausewitz and Contemporary War*, New York: Oxford University Press, 2007, pp. 55-58. Echevarria is more in tune with the master than am I on this arguably important issue. To march in step with Clausewitz is not necessarily to ensure correctness, but usually it is intellectually safer than the alternative.

33. "The political object—the original motive for the war—will thus determine both the military objective to be reached and the amount of effort it requires." Clausewitz, p. 81. Warfare is instrumental force that should have political meaning or else it would be something other than warfare. However, this political sense cannot somehow achieve a miraculous change in the violent nature of what is done on its behalf.

34. See the excellent discussion in Coates, *The Ethics of War*, especially p. 60.

35. Clausewitz, p. 605.

36. Joseph S. Nye, Jr., *Soft Power: The Means to Success in World Politics*, New York: Public Affairs, 2004, p. 5.

37. Clausewitz, p. 75.

38. Nye, *The Paradox of American Power*, p. 9.

39. *Ibid.*, p. 11.

40. *Ibid.*

41. Legends need to be related to some factual past, myths do not.

42. An interesting historical (1920s and 1930s) study of cultural pessimism is that of Richard J. Overy, *The Morbid Age: Britain and the Crisis of Civilization*, London, UK: Penguin Books, 2010.

43. For the wonderful term "cultural thoughtways," I am indebted to Ken Booth, *Strategy and Ethnocentrism*, London, UK: Croom Helm, 1979, p. 14.

44. See Paul Kennedy, *The Rise and Fall of the Great Powers: Economic Change and Military Conflict from 1500 to 2000*, New York: Random House, 1987; John J. Mearsheimer, *The Tragedy of Great Power Politics*, New York: W. W. Norton, 2001; and Jeremy Black, *Great Powers and the Quest for Hegemony: The World Order Since 1500*, Abingdon, MA: Routledge, 2008.

45. See Colin S. Gray, *National Security Dilemmas: Challenges and Opportunities*, Washington, DC: Potomac Books, 2009, Chap. 6.

46. Porter, *Military Orientalism*, is right in its critique, but only up to a point. See also the remarkable, culturally rich memoir, Pete Blaber, *The Mission, the Men, and Me: Lessons from a Former*

Delta Force Commander, New York: Berkeley Caliber, 2008. Both books are well written, but the latter has the added virtue of being a highly entertaining read, as well as a military cultural and tactical gold mine.

47. Francis Fukuyama, *The End of History and the Last Man*, New York: The Free Press, 1992. Also see Michael Mandelbaum, *The Ideas that Conquered the World: Peace, Democracy, and Free Markets in the Twenty-First Century*, New York: Public Affairs, 2002.

48. Agree with it or not, Samuel P. Huntington, *The Clash of Civilizations and the Remaking of World Order*, New York: Simon and Schuster, 1996, is a significant book that addresses some very large and enduring questions.

49. Coates, *The Ethics of War*, pp. 50-51.

50. In the apposite words of historian Jeremy Black, "Powerful states, such as China, India and Russia, expect to dominate their neighbours and do not appreciate opposition to this aspiration, as Russia has demonstrated in the Caucasus in the 1990s and 2000s — for example, in its aggressive policy towards Georgia." *Great Powers and the Quest for Hegemony*, p. 231.

51. For a classic, indeed, classical, formal presentation of the relevant geometrical geostrategic logic, see Kautilya, *The Arthashastra*, L. N. Rangarajan, trans., New Delhi, India: Penguin Books India, 1992, pp. 551-563.

52. See Paul Kennedy, *The Rise of Anglo-German Antagonism, 1860-1914*, London, UK: George Allan and Unwin, 1980; and Porter, *Military Orientalism*, especially Chap. 3 (on Western views of imperial Japan).

53. Thucydides, *The Landmark Thucydides: A Comprehensive Guide to The Peloponnesian War*, Robert B. Strassler, Rev. trans., New York: The Free Press, 1996; Nye, *Soft Power*.

54. See Gray, *The Strategy Bridge*, Chap. 1.

55. Thucydides, p. 43.

56. This regrettably unavoidable thesis underpins Colin S. Gray, *War, Peace, and International Relations: An Introduction to Strategic History*, Abingdon, MA: Routledge, 2007.

57. Not all the indicators of official Western attitudes toward the use of force are negative. For example, it was agreeable to read that despite the popularity of the view that we cannot kill our way to victory in Afghanistan, Britain's SAS, at least, have certainly been allowed to do their best to accomplish just that. See Thomas Harding and Ben Farmer, "SAS kills Taliban 'on an industrial scale'," *The Daily Telegraph* (London, UK), September 1, 2010, p. 13. The killing or other removal from the action of important enemy cadres is vital for success in counterinsurgency (COIN). Of course, COIN is about politics, and in the absence of a suitable political framework for the use of force, victory is not achievable. However, even in pervasively political COIN, the enemy leadership needs to be militarily disabled by much well-targeted physical elimination. Leadership is a key to insurgents' success.

58. See Gray, "Moral Advantage, Strategic Advantage?" for detailed explanation and argument.

59. Michael Burleigh, *Moral Combat: A History of World War II*, London, UK: HarperPress, 2010, is a powerful recent contribution to the literature.

60. See Christopher Coker, *Waging War Without Warriors? The Changing Culture of Military Conflict*, Boulder, CO: Lynne Rienner Publishers, 2002; and *The Warrior Ethos: Military Culture and the War on Terror*, Abingdon, MA: Routledge, 2007.

61. See Rune Henriksen, "Warriors in Combat—What Makes People Actively Fight in Combat?"*The Journal of Strategic Studies,* Vol. 30, No. 2, April 2007, pp. 187-223. Also highly relevant is the classic study-memoir by J. Glenn Gray, *The Warriors: Reflections on Men in Battle*, New York: Harper and Row, 1967.

62. Edward N. Luttwak, *Strategy: The Logic of War and Peace*, Rev. Ed., Cambridge, MA: The Belknap Press of Harvard University Press, 2001, p. xii. Since first reading this book, I have come to appreciate more and more how right Luttwak is in his insistence on the importance of paradox and irony in strategy.

U.S. ARMY WAR COLLEGE

Major General Gregg F. Martin
Commandant

*****

STRATEGIC STUDIES INSTITUTE

Director
Professor Douglas C. Lovelace, Jr.

Director of Research
Dr. Antulio J. Echevarria II

Author
Dr. Colin S. Gray

Director of Publications
Dr. James G. Pierce

Publications Assistant
Ms. Rita A. Rummel

*****

Composition
Mrs. Jennifer E. Nevil